MW01227360

1

Zombies!

According to Bubba

(Large Print)

Written by

Vernon Gillen

Also known as

Bubba

ISBN #

978-1496190512

Proofread by

KG

Dedication

I dedicate this book to all of you that really believe that the Necro
Mortosis Virus is real and that at least some governments have it as a weapon.
It is your work that have educated the rest of us.

To the reader

Everything written in these pages are of my own views and ideas; what I believe to be true. Facts as I took from research are listed as such but, keep in mind that the Necro Mortosis Virus could be a big hocks passed on from the government to confuse us. It would not be the first time our government has done this. With this in mind I ask that you do your own research but; research the Necro Mortosis Virus not the zombie virus. Researching the zombie virus or "T" Virus will only give you information on zombie gamers and no facts.

Contents

Introduction to

In my third novel in the Texas Under Siege series subtitled, *The Necro Mortosis Virus*, I tell all I know about the virus as I use it in the novel. However; what I wrote in that novel and, what I write in this book are a combination of facts that I learned on line and my beliefs in what is true and not true. After writing the third novel I started researching the Necro Mortosis Virus even more. I really do believe that at least the United States, Russia, and China have this virus as a weapon and that possibly, the Bilderbergs and Illuminati organizations do as well. Other countries such as North Korea and Iran also might have it.

I say that the information in this book are my beliefs because actually, no one knows everything about it except those that will not talk under punishment of death. You know what kind of death I am talking about. Suicide; shot in the back thirteen times. The governments that have this virus as a weapon do not want the information to get out there about it. So just how do they down play any information that gets out as being true? That is simple. It happens in two ways.

First, the person that talked comes up missing, never to be seen again. Second, the government plants all kinds of false information out there with some of it being just plane stupid. Our government is really good about that. Who do you think started the zombie craze in the United States; a couple of kids? Do you really think that two unknown kids can get anything so popular right now started? That takes money, many people working on it, and time.

So, that all means that some information out there is true but, you have to think about it and use you brain. Think about what your reading about the virus. Come to think of it, it does help to use a little imagination. This virus does sound like something out of a bad novel or comic book. Of course; my novel is not bad or a comic book but; the virus does exist or, at least I believe it does. That is what you have to remember as you read this book. Everything in this book is what I believe to be true along with facts that I have learned through research.

Many times I will wrote something in this book and then say

that I do not believe it. That does not mean that you will not believe it. I do ask that you think about what I wrote and then come up with your own ideas. If you agree with what I wrote then great. If you do not then it is still great. The main thing is to think about it.

In my third novel I mention many ideas; some of which I just was not sure of at the time. But, the novel is a fiction; educational book so, what the; heck: right?

You can find all of my novels and books on Amazon.com .

Chapter 1

How the Virus Works

First of all let me help you to feel a bit better about the Necro Mortosis Virus. It is not airborne. At least that is what so called; "scientist" say. They say that it can only be transmitted by an exchange of bodily fluids. In other words, any fluid that comes from a zombie, any fluids at all, and it gets into a cut on you or in your mouth or in your eyes will infect you. But I say that you can get it through the air as well.

Here is your first question. You can catch other viruses by breathing them in so, how is this virus any different?

I saw a movie one time where in part of it, a man looked up just in time for a drop of fluid to drop down from a dead (no longer moving) zombie. It hit him in the eye and he immediately knew that he was infected. In the movie he turned in minutes.

Now this brings up something that I do not believe. I do not believe that this transfer of fluids will kill you and then you turn. I believe that you would only be infected and would be able to infect others if you transfer your bodily fluids to someone not infected. In other word; there should be no more sex or even kissing once you get infected. You may still be alive but, you're a walking death sentence for anyone around you. You might want to start wearing something that will tell others that your infected. Again; this is just my belief.

I might suggest that all living infected people start wearing a simple <u>RED</u> arm band. This band should be easily seen from at least one hundred yards. On the other hand this red arm band will get you shot very quickly. Keep in mind that if you see someone wearing a red armband you should not shoot them. They are just like you except that they are infected. How you like someone to pop you just because you were unlucky enough to get infected. Just don't kiss them.

Once bitten on the leg or arm, that leg or arm can be cut off to save you from becoming infected but, it must be done quickly. In other words you cannot take your time and get knocked out before the cutting starts. A friend or, you can do it yourself, must chop off the arm or leg with an ax, machete, or anything else that is heavy and sharp. Remember that you must cut through that big bone as well as the flesh. Then you must cauterize the "stump" as quickly as you can to stop the bleeding.

Cauterizing the end of the arm or leg can easily be done with a hot burning log from the fire but, this is usually only good in the movies. The main thing is to stop the bleeding. If you can do it another way then I suggest you do it. Burns get infected more easily than any other type of wound. However; if a burning limb from a fire is all you have then you might want to take the chance. At least you will not be infected by the Necro Mortosis Virus.

Remember when I said that I do not believe that a bite will kill you but, only infect you? Keep this in mind before cutting off an arm or leg. I would rather live infected with the virus than to chop off my arm making it much harder to fight and stay alive. I can always have some one ready to put a bullet in my head if I die in another way. Now that is a friend.

Burning or cauterizing a bit will not remove the virus. You will only have a bad burn that may get badly infected. You will still have the virus unless you remove the virus infected limb quick enough.

According the scientist that work for other governments this is how the virus works once your bitten. I cannot explain why I believe that an infected person does not die but, look at the TV show

"The Walking Dead". Everyone is infected but, they only die after being bitten. I believe that a bitten person is only infected but, when you do die from a gunshot or, whatever then the virus in you will turn you into a zombie. Of course this is only what I believe.

According to these scientist; as a zombie's body fluids enter your body from a bite the virus enters the cytoplasm part of your cells. Once there the shell of the virus opens and releases a ribonucleic acid. The virus does this as your blood travels through the body and to all of the organs including the brain.

Once inside the cerebral cortex (front of the brain) the virus attacks the axons which connect the neurons in your cells. The axons are surrounded by fatty insulating sheath called myelin. This is used as an energy source for the virus to feed on. This is what a growing number of scientist now believe tricks the brain into believing that it's body has died. The body then goes into shock fallowed by slow and painful mortification and necrosis. These scientist go on to say that death of the body happens within four to forty-eight hours. The brain is somehow still alive.

Here is where I get off of the train. These scientist say that the virus tricks the brain into killing it's own body without letting the brain itself die. If the body is dead then how does it move around, eat when it can, and carry nutrition to the brain; nutrition that the virus needs to feed on? I admit that a lot of this I do not understand but, after finishing my research I still do not believe that you can die from the bit from a zombie. You will only become infected.

One web site that I read said that once the virus gets into your blood system it sits dormant; waiting for you to die of a gunshot or in any other way. When the blood is no longer flowing it cools and that triggers the virus to enter the blood cells. But let me continue with what these scientist are telling us.

The virus continues to feed on the brain's myelin coating which actually kills the body but, then reanimates it four to forty-eight hours later. The body moves around looking for food to feed the virus. This is why the zombie feeds on warm meat and blood or; the living.

The source of nutrition required by the virus is Aphion A and Betax

B which is only found in warm blood and warm meat. This explains why they do not feed on each other.

I do believe that this is how it works <u>after</u> you die of a gunshot or in another way but, not until then. I do believe that the virus remains in your bloodstream as dormant as possible until it senses the cooling of the blood. Therefore; it is my belief that you cannot die from a bit from a zombie but, you will only become infected. This should not bother you unless you love sex. I don't know who does but. At my age I think I forgot what sex is but, I don't think I'll go there. That would be something for another book.

For what it is worth to you; I found three web sites that told me the same thing as I wrote above and only the one other site that said the virus lays dormant until it feels the blood getting cooler.

Above I wrote that the virus stays dormant until the blood cools from not moving. Then the virus dumps into the bloodstream. Why does it do this if the blood is not moving? How is the virus suppose to get to the brain? I believe that the heart starts pumping again as some of the other senses and organs start working again but. I will cover that later.

You might want to be careful if you live in the northern states in the winter and you get bitten. If you get cold and your infected then; well; you might want to keep a friend handy; someone that cares enough about you to not let you change.

Chapter 2

How Zombies Might Look & Act;

Although the brain of a zombie is forced into staying alive the body still decays or; rots. We already know that some of the organs must stay alive to carry nourishment to the brain as it eats but, that is probably all. Therefore the body will not look bad at first but, look out later.

It takes a few days before the body starts to smell depending on the weather. If it is cold then decomposition will take longer to start and the body itself will last longer before falling apart.

If you live in the south like I do

and it is in the summer then once a body turns (into a zombie) it will start to smell rather fast. Give the zombie in the hot southern summer a day; maybe two at most and you will smell it coming before you see it.

Also consider the rain. As rain washes away particles of a rock to slowly grind it down it will also wash away the skin of a zombie first. Then it would only be a matter of days before the constant rain washes away pieces of the muscles used to enable the zombie to move around.

In the northern states, in the winter, you will see the same destruction of the zombie body but, in a different way. As snow or freezing rain sticks to the body of a zombie it will freeze any exposed skin. When enough of the snow or freezing rain piles up, it will break off and fall to the ground; with chunks of skin and flesh stuck to it.

Although the heart must pump to carry nourishment to the brain I believe that the zombie's body would still be cold or, at least cool. This will help in how much of the body will freeze and fall off with any snow or freezing rain.

Also keep in mind that although the zombie must feed, that does not mean that it has plenty to eat. Having more to eat would heat the body up some but, after a short while there would be less and less to eat. With nothing to eat for, maybe days the body of the zombie would only have the friction of the blood flowing through the veins and arteries to warm it up any. Even living humans will freeze so, I believe that a zombie would freeze quicker and be unable to move. This would be good if you live in the northern states in the winter. As the zombie is frozen it cannot attack you. Just remove its head as it lays there looking up at you and it will not bother anyone else later.

So, how fast the body rots to the point that the zombie can no longer hurt you depends on where you live, what type of weather your having at the time, and how long you can stay away from them. That is the main thing. Stay away from them.

However; expect the most horrible sight that you have ever seen. You will see things that even Hollywood could not think of. Well; I have seen some really good zombie movies but, not what I know I will see when the virus is unleashed on us.

The best movie that I can think

of right now is one in which a few young people got together with a few people in town, one camera and a budget so low that no one got paid. Of course I am talking about "*Night of the Living Dead*". In this movie (the first one) they did not hold anything back. Although still in black and white as I write this, the movie shows zombies eating entrails of the person they caught and killed and walking away with human guts as they fight for their piece of the warm meat. To this day, although movie makers try to keep us grossed out they do not show what it would really be like. However; this movie does not show what zombies would really look like.

I am a big fan of *The Walking Dead* series. Now in this series they show what the zombies might look like. They show skeletons walking around with just enough flesh on the body to make it believable that it could still walk around. Maybe they should have more bones showing than they show now. Still; I suggest that if you believe that the zombie virus or, Necro Mortosis Virus is real, you watch this series. You will learn a lot as I can see that this series must research their work before adding anything in their show.

By now you must be asking how long the body of a zombie can keep walking. Under perfect conditions with the weather being perfect for the zombie; maybe about ninety days. So called experts on line give this number as it takes about ninety days for the body to break down to the point that it could no longer walk. But; is it safe to walk close to them. I say no.

In my third novel I give four types of zombies and here they are.

<u>Stalkers</u>: I used the word stalkers because I needed a name that had not been used by anyone else. In my third novel in the *Texas Under Siege* series a Stalker is the first stage of a zombie as it is able to walk. Once it sees you it stalks you. Therefore the name; Stalkers.

<u>Crawlers</u>: In my third novel a stalker reaches a point when it can no longer walk and therefore crawls on all fours. The muscles in it's legs can no longer carry the weight of the body and it falls to the ground. From this point it is still able to crawl. Of course this is a novel and not reality.

<u>Sliders</u>: When the body of a zombie finally decays enough that it

can not even crawl it falls to the ground and begins to slide around like a snake or worm. It might roll from side to side but, nothing it does will be vary fast. They might lay motionless but, still be able to reach out and grab your leg as you walk by. Do not underestimate the strength that a zombie might have; even a slider. A sliding will also quickly tear off much of the remaining flesh as it moves around.

<u>Biters</u>: When the body of a zombie can no longer even slide around then it becomes a Biter. Keep in mind that the virus is in the brain and therefore the head is still alive. If you step close enough to the Biter's mouth then it might be able to bite you. If you are burning bodies, which would be the best way to dispose of the massive amount of dead bodies that you will

have, then watch how you pick up a body or, severed head.

Severing the head of a zombie will not kill it; only the body. The head remains alive until it finally reaches a point that even it rots to far and, even with the help of the virus, it cannot stay alive. More likely it will die from malnutrition first. Remember that unless the zombie feeds it dies and a head cannot feed without the help of the arms and legs. Of course some of you might keep a pet, human head and carefully feed it now and then but, please try not to do this. The undead were once human. Treat them with respect.

I believe that the zombie will walk for about sixty to ninety day before it falls to the ground. It might crawl for another week depending on the weather again. By this time the body will have decayed enough that I do not think it will be a slider for more than a few days. I give it another day or so as a biter. That is about three and a half months of reanimation after the human dies.

Also keep in mind that as a loved one dies they need their brain destroyed as fast as possible. Once they are reanimated you might not even know that they are a zombie as they walk up to you for a bite. Sick loved ones need to be watched to make sure that they do not die and become reanimated. Remember that anyone you think might be reanimated cannot answer questions or speak in any way. So, if they answer your question, no matter how bad they look, try not to shoot them in the head.

Just after reanimation the

zombie will not have sunken in eyes, dark circles around the eyes, or anything else that might give you a hint that they have turned. Do not trust that a loved one that has turned will not hurt you. They are no longer your loved one and will eat, and infect, you as soon as they can.

I suggest that anyone around you that is deathly ill should be tied to their bed. Zombies are dead and will not have the brains (no fun intended) to untie a knot. Again; keep someone there to watch them anyway. Look at it this way. Would you rather have to shoot your loved one in the head after they die and before they turn or have them turn into a monster. They will not be suffering as they feel no pain but; do you really want to see them that way? However; make sure that they are infected with the Necro Mortosis Virus and not just sick with a cold or the flue. Simply wait until they die and then shoot them in the head.

However; because they do not feel pain, if you have a pair of handcuffs, handcuffing then to the bed might not be good enough. They might actually sever their arm some how and get away. Handcuffs can easily cut off a hand if they are pulled on hard enough. If this happens at night and you're asleep then you could be joining them on a "zombie walk-a-bout". Of course this would come after a lot of pain of them chewing on you.

Like I said; just expect to see the worst thing you ever saw in your life. A zombie is no longer your loved one. They are a monster that will eat you alive if given half of a chance to do it. I can not even imagine how that must feel. To be eaten alive; having my entrails pulled out of me as I watch and scream in pain. And then to know that, as I lay there unable to stop the extreme pain, it is a loved one that is doing this to me.

As for me; I own a pistol and will have no problem using it if I need to. Above all things; I will survive.

Chapter 3

The Facts About the Virus

Here are some facts about the Necro Mortosis Virus that I collected from over twenty web sites that I took seriously. My comments on each one are in Italics.

1. The virus is transferred only through an exchange of body fluids.

I do not believe that a bit will kill you. You will only be infected. I also believe that the virus, like all other viruses, are airborne. However; not being an expert on viruses; I could be wrong about this virus.

2. The virus can be contracted through the sharing of needles.

Again this is one way to transfer

fluids from one person to another. Of course this can only happen if one of the people sharing a needle is infected.

3. As this is written there is no known antidote for the Necro Mortosis Virus. The virus can be transmitted by having sex with an infected partner.

If you think that giving or receiving a BJ will not get you infected then you had better think again. Even a person receiving this "sexual pleasure" can get the virus from saliva of an infected person; just like with HIV.

There is one antidote for this virus. It is called a bullet.

4. The virus is not airborne.

I believe that you can inhale the virus as it is stuck to water vapors such as fog or low clouds. This maybe a highly specialized virus but, *it is still a virus.*

5. Only infected people will reanimate after death.

This is one of the reasons that I believe that the virus remains dormant until you die and start getting cold.

6. Non-infected people or, people who die of natural causes will not turn and rise as a zombie.

As long as you never get bitten or in any other way get infected then you will not turn after you die. You cannot turn if you do not have the virus. However; I believe that you can get infected from the air so, you and everyone around you would be infected.

7. Severing an infected arm or leg will not remove the infection unless done within the first few seconds after being bitten.

Again I say this but; why chop off

an arm or leg when the infection will not kill and turn you anyway? Doing this will only make you more dependent on others to help you do things. Removing an arm or leg brings your survival chances down to about 50% or less. If we all are infected by the air born virus then cutting off a limb would not help. Just take care of the wound as you would any dog bite. Yes you will be infected but, you will remain more independent. Burning the wound will not help you do anything but, get a nasty infection.

8. Animals that are infected and die do not re-animate.

Now here is where I get off of the next train. How does the virus know if it is in a human or dog? I believe that there will be infected animals that will attack humans just as the infected humans that die will. An *infected brain is an infected brain. A zombie is still a zombie whether it has two or four legs.*

Chapter 4

Symptoms of the Necro Mortosis Virus

Although I do not believe that a bit from a zombie will kill you the information that I have written below is important for you to know. I could be wrong in my beliefs but, to be honest, I am never wrong. My x-wife would disagree but, that is just her. I might not be right all of the time but, I am never wrong. Incase you have not figured it out I am joking. Please don't send me an e-mail about thinking that I am really never wrong.

According to the almost twenty web sites that I took to be

serious enough to read, I came up with these symptoms of a person that has been bitten. Although I do not believe that a bit from an infected person or zombie will kill you they will infect you. Some of these symptoms still may happen in a bitten person. I believe that after going through some illness when bitten, it is just the virus being introduced into the body. Like any drug you will have side affects. A bitten person may go through some of these side effects, if not all of these. Over ten of the web sites that I researched agreed that an infected person will reanimate within four to forty eight hours after the infected person dies.

<u>First Stage</u>: symptoms feel like the flue. The infected person will have migraines, hot flashes, and

aching muscles.

Second Stage: is fallowed by chills, some disorientation, extreme loss of coordination, and a slowing of the heart beat. The person may fall into a coma, have a stroke, or heart failure. The person dies.

Although I do believe that a bitten person will get somewhat sick I do not believe that many will die just from the bite. The introduction of the virus into the body might cause some to have a stroke or heart attack. I credit this to the person not being strong. In other words I believe that the person that dies from a bit must have a bad heart. They were to weak in the first place to withstand the shock of the virus entering their body. Only these people will die after being bitten. This will probably happen to older people that get bitten. Introduction of this virus will defiantly be a shock to anyone's body. The weak ones might die from the bite.

In the <u>Third Stage</u> Necrosis and mortification will fallow. The body is reanimated within four to forty-eight hours.

When a family member dies you have at least four hours to crush or pierce their head. Destroy the brain. Only removing the head will leave you with a loved one's head trying to bite you. The brain must be destroyed.

It is the part that said "Studied Subjects" that got my attention. I really believe that the United States, Russia, and China have this virus as a weapon already. Therefore; I believe that at least all three of these countries are studying this virus. So if the United States is studying this virus then where are their test subjects coming from? Do you really believe that people actually volunteer to become a zombie?

Have you ever heard about our children being used as human test subjects back in the fifties? Of course but, most of us brushed it off as just a story. How many of you that might be around fifty to sixty years old remember fluoride being rubbed on our teeth in school. The government said that it was good for our teeth. Now we learn that it weakens the mind. This makes us all "sheeple" (sheep/people), a combination of people and sheep. Makes you wonder what else our loving government is doing to us.

Look at it this way. I remember the nurse stabbing a q-tip with fluoride on it and maybe touching one tooth. Now how was that suppose to help all of my teeth? Helping my teeth was not the true reason for the government doing this. If the government will use our children for test subjects then why not for testing this virus?

How often do we hear of missing homeless people? We never do because they are homeless. But hundreds each year really do come up missing in the United States. Could our government be grabbing the homeless for testing this virus and other weapons? Back in the 1940's our government came up with how radiation effected the human body. Just how did they know? From wooden dummies in a fake town in the blast area? If you believe that then you are very gullible.

Chapter 5

Do They Breath

I am not sure what I can believe on this. In all movies and in The Walking Dead series all of the zombies make noises. Of course this is Hollywood. But, it does make since that they would make some sounds.

As their bodies rot, gasses would escape every now and then. If they digest meat for nourishment then it would make since that the brain also needs oxygen.

I believe that some parts of the brain also work other than just the cerebral cortex. The word cerebral means the front of the brain and the word <u>cortex</u> means the outer layer of a solid organ or part of the body; the outer covering of the kidney or brain cerebral cortex.

The cerebral or, front of the brain is where you get your personality. Do you really think a zombie will have any kind of a personality? Well; lets go on.

Therefore; if the virus enters the cortex of the front part of the brain (the cerebellum) then why not the cortex of other organs to keep them alive as well? Therefore I believe that many parts of the body might be kept alive for the purpose of enabling the body to move and process nutrition and oxygen.

So yes; I do believe that they breath. But, can they walk under water to invade an island? If the body of a zombie needs oxygen then my answer would have to be no;

they cannot walk for long under water. Although a zombie might enter the water and try to travel under water I believe that they would die a second death within; or lets say; less than twenty feet; just like a living human. Zombies walk slow and, by time they walk that distance then the brain would be dead from lack of oxygen. Zombie or human; the brain still needs oxygen.

Chapter 6

How Do Zombies Know the Living From the Dead

With a zombie being cold or, maybe warm they might be able to sense warmer bodies. This means that when you see a human walking among zombies then they are just making another movie.

Another way that the zombie might know the living from the dead is through smell. Although some of us might smell a bit bad after working we do not have a rotting smell to us. Well; most of us don't. Maybe a zombie can smell this lack of a rotting smell.

In the last chapter I mentioned

that I believe that the zombie does in fact breath. Therefore they should be able to smell. Also keep in mind that if other parts of the brain is stimulated into working then why not the part that has to do with being able to smell.

Look at it this way. If only a part of the brain is alive to keep the body moving then how would the zombie know humans from other zombies? So, my belief makes since. They must be able to smell us out.

As they walk the zombie also seem to be able to see where they are walking. Although their eyes are glazed over at first and then covered with dirt and dust they can still see a little. If this part of the brain works then why not the part that controls smell.

Now getting back to the eyes. I believe that their eyes are glazed over after a few hours of being reanimated. This would be caused from them not blinking and lubricating the eyeball. It dries out and gets foggy. Over time dirt and dust covers the eyeball making it even harder for the zombie to see where they are going.

For this reason I believe that this is why zombies might walk in groups. It is easier to see a group of shadows moving than trying to find your own way around.

However; this does not help a zombie to find you but, it might help them to find food as a group.

If a zombie can see and smell then why not hear? In my third novel I very slowly walked up to a zombie with only a fence between us. It did not know I was there until I quickly moved. Only then did it hear and see me as a shadow. Even then it tried to grab me as it did not know that there was a fence between us. The fence did not move and therefore; it could not see, smell, or hear it. It only knew that it could not grab me for some reason but, it continued to try to grab me until I shot it.

Now we have gathered that a zombie can smell, hear, and see so, why should the other senses not work as well? Lets take the sense of being able to feel. I believe that if a zombie grabs or brushes up against you then they can feel your being warmer than it. It might grab for you then but, maybe only then. I do not really believe that a zombie can feel the heat coming from your body just by being close to you. Also consider this.

If your living in the warm south and in the summer then you might see a few zombies attacking a few other warm inanimate objects or, maybe each other. You might see them attacking steel beams, cars and trucks, or even a tree or two. I believe that after a while they would learn that these things are not for eating. So if you wanted to take cover in a car or pickup as a group of zombies came through you would be safe as long as you did not move or make a sound. As the group of zombies walked passed you then an individual zombie would as well. They would not be able to smell, hear, or feel you as long as you were in that car or truck. If you remained still then they would not see you either.

One more sense remains. The sense of taste. It is very simple. If they taste you then you messed up someplace and you are being eaten.

Ouch! Wake up Dumb-ass. You're being eaten.

As with the other senses I do believe that they can taste things as well. However; as they would be very hungry they would not care what you tasted like. Fresh meat and blood might even be appealing to them. Also, the drive to feed might over power this one sense. This is a powerful virus and could do most anything like blocking at least one sense. However; I believe that the zombie's body would need and use the other four senses in order to find food; in order to find you.

Of course no one knows everything about the Necro Mortosis Virus but, you might want to assume that they can find you much easier than the movies let us believe.

Chapter 7

Types of Zombies

For every serious web site that is written on zombies there are different types. Every webmaster gives names for the zombies but, no one seems to give the same names. Well here we go. I am about to do the same thing.

I will give types of zombies to consider which I used in my third novel. They are Stalkers, Crawlers, Sliders, and Biters. I mentioned these earlier in this book but I will go more into the definition in this chapter.

1. <u>Stalkers</u>: I had to use a name in

my book that no one had ever used so, I went with stalkers. A Stalker is a zombie that just recently reanimated. They are able to walk and grab things. Most all zombies start off this way but, some people will be paralyzed; maybe be in wheelchairs when they died. A paralyzed person would not have the ability to walk even after reanimating.

A zombie that is in a wheelchair would not have the coordination or remember how to use it. They would probably sit there until they died a second death; this time from malnutrition. They would starve to death.

They might fall out of their wheelchairs and then become what I call Crawlers or Sliders. Only in this way would they be able to move around. A paraplegic before death would not be able to move at all and, if it fell from it's wheelchair it would probably become a biter.

2. <u>Crawlers</u>: The reanimated body or, zombie, would only be able to walk around for about ninety days or, three months at the most. At this point their bodies would be decayed enough that the legs would no longer be able to carry the weight of the body. At this point they would fall to the ground.

Once on the ground the virus would still be giving them the drive to feed. Unable to feed unless they found something close they would die the second death. Without nourishment the brain dies. A Crawler would not last more than two weeks at the most unless it fed on warm meat and blood. They would only last two weeks if they had stored up enough nourishment to hold it over that long. Most Crawlers would last about a week before turning into what I call Sliders.

3. <u>Sliders</u>: Sliders are zombies that were unable to crawl anymore or never could as with someone in a wheelchair. The muscles just would not be able to carry the body any more; even crawling. Unable to at least crawl the Slider still has the drive the feed and, by this time, should be needing nourishment badly. It then slides along much like a snake or worm. It might even roll from place to place.

The only nourishment that the Slider would get is if warm meat is dropped right in front of it.

4. <u>Biter</u>: A Biter is a zombie which

can no longer even slide from one place to another. It might not even be able to move it's arms or legs at all but, the head is still alive.

Caution needs to be taken when burning these dead zombie. A Biter may look dead causing you to let your guard down. You could still get bitten depending on how you picked it up. Always assume that a dead zombie could still be a Biter. Before picking then up to throw into a fire remove the head and drag the body to the fire. Then pick up the heads by the hair, if it has any. You can also grab it by the ears unless they are rotting to bad for that. A shovel or pitchfork would be useful here.

I would say that a Biter might not remain alive or, the head might remain alive for another three days. By this time the brain has not had any or, not much nourishment for a while. It's organs that were also reanimated started failing a few weeks earlier so, it might not even be getting oxygen anymore.

Take care when walking among dead zombies. Even stepping to close to the mouth of a Biter could cause you to get bitten. Remember that Biters may sill have the ability to move some or, they may not be able to move at all. Because the arms of a Biter cannot hold the body up anymore does not mean that it cannot reach out and grab your leg as you walk by. It just might reach out for a bit to eat.

Also consider this if I am wrong about the Necro Mortosis Virus being air born. If you walk by a biter and it reaches out and scratches you then the bodily fluids on its hand would infect you through the scratch. Sever the head and the arms will not be able to move.

Chapter 8

Is There a Cure

There have been studies in Berlin, Germany that are proving not to be far from a cure for the Necro Mortosis Virus but, as I write this, there is no cure yet. At least there is no cure that anyone wants to let the public know about. Keep in mind that if the Bilderbergs or Illuminati have the cure then they will never let us know. How would they be able to achieve their goal of world domination if everyone had a cure for the virus? They would keep this cure for themselves.

Any government that might have the cure for the virus would

never admit that the virus even existed anyway and therefore there must not be any cure. Face it. The governments of the world, including the United States, do not really care about their people.

In Berlin an inhibitor called XL-6 is being tested. It is suppose to interrupt the process of the virus taking over the body by preventing the virus particle from opening after it enters the blood cell and stops the manufacturing of proteins that the virus needs to continue.

If I am right that the virus remains dormant until it feels the blood cooling then this drug is useless until you actually die in some way. Like I said before. Keep a friend handy to put a bullet in your head when you die and then you will not have to worry about turning. That will be a lot cheaper than what I am sure any cure will cost you.

A research center in Florida is also working on a cure. I found two cases on U-tube that showed zombies attacking someone. I know that many of the short reports are fake and it is easy to see. However; I took the two that were from news crews; film that was taken to show on TV. I only trusted these two films.

Chapter 9

How Could the Virus be Introduced

Even if the Necro Mortosis Virus is not airborne there are still a number of ways that it can be introduced into the public.

Not being airborne means that you cannot inhale it into your lungs and get the virus into your bloodstream. Scientist say that the virus must adhere to something like food or water. It also mean that the virus cannot float in the air. So, the question is, if the virus is combined with water and released from an airplane, can we get infected by inhaling the water droplets as a vapor or mist? This is why I base my theory that the virus is in fact air born.

This means that any government can spray a large city from the air and no one would know it until the morgues started having customers leaving; if you know what I mean. Just infecting a small town would totally cover our nation within two or three months; the whole world in three months.

Of course I am sure that our government would never do this; right? They might not but, the Illuminati; a group of very rich members might. It is the goal of the Bilderbergs and the Illuminati to one day rule over the Earth. First they must reduce the population of the Earth to the point that they can rule over the survivors. Both organization are in the United States but, the Illuminati are building whole cities in the caves and limestone mines of Oklahoma, Kansas and Arkansas. Someone with the goal of ruling over the Earth might just use this virus to reduce the population to what they want.

In my third novel the Illuminati unleashes this virus on the public of the United States but, it backfired and infected them as well. Once this virus is unleashed it cannot be controlled.

So, how else might a rouge "group of people" distribute this virus. The next time you take a drink of water think about where it comes from. Many large cities reuse water from their sewer plants. That's right. Your drinking your neighbor's commode water. I know of one city, which I cannot mention, that does just this. Half of the drinking water comes from it's sewer plant. Now; this is not really bad; in a way.

I have an aquatic sewer system that my home uses. No I do not drink it but, it does spray the water in the field where my sheep enjoy very green grass. This system is also used on the space shuttles where the astronauts actually do drink their (cleaned) human waste water. It really is clean enough to drink. But, that is not what I am getting at.

It would be so easy to pour a vial of the Necro Mortosis Virus into a city's drinking water and the whole city would be infected within days. No one would know until those customers started leaving the morgue.

There is still one more method of infecting the public. When was the last time you looked at your food and saw where it came from? Chicken for example, comes from all over Texas at least; probably other places as well. I know that there are chicken farms all around where I live. But, where do all of the chickens go? Most of them are shipped alive to east Texas where they are butchered, cleaned, and packaged to send out to grocery stores all over the place.

What about beef? How many butcher yards are there in the United States? What about hogs and other meats? How many farms send in fresh produce to stores? How many of those fresh vegetables are canned? How do you know that they were not sprayed with the virus while still in the fields? Now it is going all over the world.

It would be so easy to add some of the Necro Mortosis Virus to those fresh vegetables or maybe the canned vegetables. How much food do we ship in from other countries? With as many enemies as our nation has would we know in time if they added this virus to the food they are sending to us? Do you still think your food is safe?

If a "group of people" coordinated it just right to add the virus to our food supply all over the country then at least eighty percent of the population of the United States could be infected within a week; before anyone even knew that something was going on.

Think of it this way. How many times do we hear about hair, or something else being found in a can of soup?

I buy that flat bread where you can get only eight sandwiches out of a loaf. I bought some last month and found that two of the loafs were eaten on by rats before they were even packaged. If this can slip by the bread makers then what else can?

This is why I am getting more and more into canning my own foods. I grow a garden and can what I can. I freeze the rest but, I also know that I could loose electricity and all of the food in the freezer.

The thing is; stop trusting these companies that prepare our food. Do it yourself.

I do not even want to think about what all the government is already having added to the flue shots that millions in our country get. I will not get another one again because I know what is in them. Trust me. Your flue shot is not just medication for the flue. A lot more is in that shot. If the government is doing this with the flue vaccines then what else are they messing with? You might be surprised.

Oh yes! Here is one more thing to think about. What if a "group of people" used all four of these methods at one time in order to infect the public?

We would not stand a chance.

Chapter 10

Preparing Defenses

There are many ways to prepare for this disaster of; for what ever reason the Necro Mortosis Virus is released on the public. No matter how or why the virus was introduced into the public you still are faced with surviving it. No problem unless your as dumb as an elected Democrat. Survival depends very much on your imagination.

First you need to understand that the virus keeps the zombie alive no more than three and a half months at the most. But, the virus will not just suddenly give you millions of zombies walking around.

Remember that I do not believe that the Necro Mortosis Virus in itself kills anyone that is infected. Only after you die of other causes does the infected person turn into a zombie. Anyone bleeding badly enough from a zombie attack would die and reanimate to attack someone else. In this way you might have whole areas of a city with numerous zombies walking around and attacking people. Thank God I live out in the country. The closest city to me is Waco, Texas. It is a good forty five miles away as the crow flies.

However; you might believe that the virus does kill everyone that gets infected. If you do then you might have millions of zombies suddenly walking around. Then again; if the virus is not airborne then how would so many people get infected? It would not be much of a weapon if it was not airborne which is why I believe it is. It does not matter if you take my theory or not. The Zombie Apocalypse, if that is what you want to call it, is still coming.

So how would you prepare any defenses? That depends on where you live. Keep in mind that, lets say, if you have a strong fence set up around your house. A few zombies will not be able to climb over it or push it over. But, if you have many of them leaning on that same fence then it might fall over with their combined weight.

You must first keep quiet and not move around giving them shadows to want to walk towards or all of the fences in the world will not help you.

Let me get back to fences. Any

field fence, chicken wire, or chain link fence will work as long as it is at least six feet high. Even strands of barb wire would work if you have many strands up. They had better be tight as well.

The "T" posts or wood posts would need to be at least three feet in the ground. It is important to have them deep in the ground to give the fence more strength.

You will need a way out so, a gate is important; maybe two at opposite ends of the fenced in area would be nice. These gates also give the zombies a weaker point in the fence so, make sure these are strong gates. Zombies will not know a gate from any other part of the fence but, it will be the week point in your fence so, still make them strong.

Lets say you live in or are trapped in an apartment. All

apartments have one main doorway into the building. Some have two. Block these entrances with anything you can. If this entrance is a single door then lock the door and keep away from it. If a zombie sees you then it or, they will try to get through to you. Stacking furniture in these doorways will not work for long which is why you need to make sure that the zombies do not see you in that area. If they do then they will probably push their way through fairly easily.

It would be best to drive or push a few cars in the way of these openings to your apartment building. You can close the windows but, again, if they see you in that area they could break the door windows and crawl through the car.

I suggest that you drive a couple of cars up against the opening into the building, open the door closest to you and fill the car with furniture. Full plastic garbage bags would work great here. Zombies do not have the common sense to open the door on their side and remove the furniture.

There is still the chance that the zombies will squeeze between the car and the wall of the building or even under a truck put there. Force more furniture in these areas. Again; a zombie does not have the common sense to remove the obstacle. They can only use brute force and the weight of many of them to push their way through.

I heard one man say one time that he would put sharp objects in the zombie's way. Remember that they are dead and would not feel pain so, this will not work. The ONLY thing that will work is completely blocking their way to you.

Posting a guard that can watch these areas is a great idea as well. The guard should be armed and should sit still in the shadows where he or she can watch the opening or openings without being seen. If shooting is heard from this guard then everyone in the building with a firearm should come to the opening ready for a fight. All of your lives might depend on it. One coward could get all of you killed.

I probably lost a few liberals there but, that's to bad. I can see the letters that I would get from bleeding heart liberals that bought this book. *"You shouldn't kill zombies. Their our friends."* Let's see the liberals fight off a horde of zombies with those tennis rackets they keep for home protection.

This guard should never move unless he or she has to. They should sit there watching the entrance to make sure that no zombies start actually coming through. Never shoot at a zombie that is simply pushing on the barricade. This is normal and firing at one of them will let all of them know that you are there.

Relieving the guard every now and then is a must. Some of the zombies might see this movement and start pushing on your barricade. If you built a good barricade then the new guard should just quickly sit down and be still. With nothing moving to stimulate the zombie's drive to find food then they should calm down and go about their business of finding warm meat to eat. If you did not build a good barricade then; well; good-by.

Many people, survivors of this virus will be caught with no place or not enough money to get fencing and other supplies. I suggest that you help people like this. On the other hand you cannot invite everyone into your place and have no way to feed them. However; if they are well armed and you are not then you might want to consider sharing your food for their help in defending the place.

Chapter 11

Stockpiling

Every survivalist out there knows that something is about to happen. Just look in the book of Revelations in the Bible.

You might ask what you should stockpile. It is real simple. You need to stockpile anything that you feel is important in order to live a normal life; as normal as possible anyway. Of course that is actually impossible. So what do you do? You make a mental list, maybe on paper, of anything you feel you need in order to survive any disaster that comes along.

If you live in the south then you

might want to survive a hurricane. If you live in the north then you might want to survive a blizzard. In any case you need things that will help you survive.

The way I see it you will need at least these few things in surviving any situation.

1. <u>Food</u>: In any case or situation you should have at least six months of food saved up for each person in your family. Towards the end of the six months, in a zombie situation, you might want to consider slacking off on your eating to make it last longer.

If you have zombies walking around then you will not be able to hunt even if you do live out on the country. Many of the animals could be infected and maybe no amount of cooking will kill the virus before you eat the meat. If you eat infected meat then you will be infected. On the other hand the heat used in cooking the meat would kill any germs so why not the virus as well?

2. <u>Water</u>: You cannot survive more than a few days without water. If your lucky you will do that good. If the situation is so bad that zombies are walking around then I am sure that the water company will not be working and you will not have any water coming to you.

I buy fruit juice in one gallon jugs and then wash out the empty jugs. Then I add one drop of bleach to the jug and then fill it with water. That water will still be good a year later because of the one drop of bleach I added to it and it taste just as fresh as if it came from the kitchen faucet that day.

You can buy eye droppers with a tiny bottle at any pharmacy. Use clear jugs so that you can see any colorization that might form in the form of green slime on the inside of the jug. This green slim will not harm you. In fact you can eat it.

When I was in the navy we pulled the submarine into a dry dock for some work. One day I had to go into the potable (drinking) water tank to clean it. When I dropped into the tank I was surprised to see at least six inches of this same slime in the tank. Then I was told that I was only cleaning it to keep it from building up to much. The slime actually helps to clean the water.

There was no chlorine in the submarine's water tanks but, there will be in your jug so, it should stay clear a long time.

One more thing. I know this sounds nasty but, in a survival situation it will work. If you find yourself with no water, for a short time you can drink your own urine <u>but, only yours</u>. Many of the American prisoners in Vietnam were forced to do this and not one of them died from it. I have never done this and am not looking forward to this but, I will survive. I will do this if I have to. Just thinking about this gives me a good reason to save and store up water.

3. <u>Firearms and ammunition</u>: I suggest that you have at least one rifle and one pistol for everyone old enough to fire them.

Having plenty of ammunition is a must. You do not know how long you will be hiding out in your home. You might have to run for it but, without plenty of ammunition, how far would you get?

A simple .22 caliber rifle will work on zombies but, you will find plenty of living people trying to take what you have. A .22 rifle might not be enough against them. I suggest you have one person carrying a .22 caliber rifle and you carry a AR-15 or, any other rifle that uses a .223 caliber round.

4. <u>Sheets or blankets</u>: You will need sheets or blankets to cover the windows so the zombies cannot see you. Even if you live in an upstairs apartment you do not want them seeing you. They will try to push through any blockades that you have downstairs to get to you. Remember this. Never advertise to the zombies that you are where you are. Yes, it will be a bit dark during

the days but, you will be alive.

5. <u>**Human Waste**</u>**: No this is not something that you want to store up but, you need to consider this.**

Human waste must be gotten rid of or you will have a problem with diseases. If anything have everyone use a bucket that can be emptied out of a window. This does build up and can cause diseases to enter your home. But, do what you must in order to survive.

Keep in mind what I said above about being out of water. Just remember that you can only drink your own urine and, only if you have to.

These are the basic things that I can think of but, I am sure that you can think of more. Each person will have a different list of what they

think is most important but, at least make a list and try your best to fill it.

Chapter 12

Surviving The Living

In any disaster you must also watch out for the living. Of course I am talking about the ten percent of the population that is, no matter the situation, useless trash. During any disaster they show just how evil they can get but, in a situation where about eighty percent of the population has turned into warm flesh eating "citizens" any of this trash that has survived will become even more evil. The worse the disaster the more evil they will be. They will kill you for your food and water and, a good hiding place if you have it.

These people will probably be

young, maybe from as young as twelve up to maybe thirty. Look around where you live now. What kind of people do you see within a two mile circle around your home? Always keep this in mind. Do not just shoot anyone coming around your hideout during a disaster. Some will be really good people that you might want to join you. There is safety in numbers. The more of you there are the safer you all will be.

You will know these bad people by their actions. Unfortunately; you will seldom see their actions until you get to close to run away.

When approaching any group of people you will need to sit back and watch them for a while if you can. You will hear about cults all over the place claiming that God did this. Sorry folks but, God will only judge us later on judgment day. On that day you will either go to Heaven or Hell. You will not be fighting zombies. Did I mention that I am a Christian?

As I mentioned in my third novel the United Nations came into the United States at the request of our "Marxist" president. When the Necro Mortosis Virus starts going around even the UN soldiers will get infected. As they die they will turn like anyone else. Then they will drop their weapons. As you kill the UN zombies you will be able to grab their weapons and ammunition. Face it. After a short time there will be plenty of fully automatic weapons and ammunition for them laying around. Grab a rifle, pistol, and ammunition for both.

In a time when zombies are walking around the reanimated dead will not be all you will have to worry about.

Also consider the animals. Although scientist do not believe that, after being infected with the Necro Mortosis Virus, they will reanimate, I do. Think of it this way. How does a virus know if it is in a human or animal brain?

Therefore; when the world goes to hell in a hand basket; when everything falls apart, you will be dealing with human and animal zombies as well as bad guys. Because I do not believe that everyone will be infected at one time you will have at least three months of hunkering down in your home. If your quiet then the human zombies will not be bothering you. But as time goes by more and more people will become zombies by one way or another. Therefore; you will be waiting a lot more than just the ninety days for a zombie to die a second death. As they die others are just becoming zombies and you will have ninety days of waiting them out. Then others become zombies and; see what I mean? You must have a lot of food and water saves up.

Now! What about the animal that have turned? When alive their ears were a lot better than ours. Just how much better will the ears of an animal zombie be than a human zombie? Will they still be better or just as good?

Then you will still have the human trash that I mentioned. I am sure that they will try to enter your home if they think you have anything that they need or just want.

The best thing to do is blockade your home or apartment and get ready to fight. Remember that as you blockaded your home good enough to keep out the humans and human zombies, is it good enough to keep out the animal zombies? Do you really think that you can keep out even the mice?

Who knows. Maybe we are all doomed and we just do not know it yet.

Final Comments

I researched the Necro Mortosis Virus for almost six months and only found about fifteen serious web sites on it. I encourage you to do your own research but, do not research "The Zombie Virus" or "the T Virus". These sites are mostly just zombie gamers. If your going to research this then at least try to keep it real.

I do believe that at least the United States, Russia, and China have the Necro Mortosis Virus as a weapon. One web site said that North Korea and Iran have offered Russia, which sales anything to anyone, millions in gold for this virus but, Russia refused. It seems that Russia is so scared of this virus that they do not want rogue nations with spoiled brat leaders, like in

North Korea, to have it. Keep that in mind. However; did the writer of that web site make that information up or was it true? I guess we will never know.

This virus as a weapon really bothers me. Nuke me if you want; vaporize my body in a millisecond if you want. Just do not make me walk the Earth as a zombie. I do not believe the virus will kill me. I believe what three other web sites said about it; that the virus circulates through the body in your warm blood but, lays dormant until you die and your body gets cooler. The virus in your brain will then do what it does and the virus in and around your organs will do what it does. I will not worry if I get the virus but, will steer clear of it as well; if I can. For me; if this virus is released I think I will keep a friend nearby to put a bullet in my head when I die. I have a good friend that will do that.

Do you?

Other Publications of

Vernon Gillen

Below is a list of my other novels and books that have been published.

Novels

1. "Texas Under Siege 1."
Tale of a Survival Group Leader.
After a man is voted as the leader of his survival group in Texas a self proclaimed Marxist president asked the United Nations troops to come in and settle down the civil unrest. The civil unrest was really nothing but Americans that complained about how he ran the

country.

2. "Texas Under Siege 2."
The Coming Storms.
The young group leader continues to fight when the countries that made up the United Nations troops in the United States decided to take over parts of the country for their own country's to control.

3. "Texas Under Siege 3."
The Necro Mortorses Virus.
As the group leader continues to fight the UN he learns that an old organization really controlled everything. They were known as the Bilderbergs. Tired of the resistance in Texas they release the Necro Mortorses virus also known as the zombie virus.

4. "Texas Under Siege 4."
250 Years Later.

This novel jumps 250 years into the future where the Bilderbergs are still living with modern technology while the other people have been reduced to living like the American Indians of the early 1800's. One of these young man stands up and fights the Bilderbergs with simples pears and arrows.

Other Books

1. "Carnivores of Modern Day Texas."

A study of the animals in Texas that will not only kill you but in most cases will eat you.

2. "Zombies; According to Bubba"
After studying the Necro

Mortises virus for my novel *Texas Under Siege 3*, I realized that I had a great deal of information on it. After finishing the novel I wrote this book leaving the reader to make their own decision.

Unpublished

A great deal goes into publishing a novel or book that takes time. After I write a novel I have someone proofread it. Then I have to find an artist to draw the cover picture which is hard to do. Actually finding an artist is easy but finding one that I can afford is not so easy. Then the novel or book has to be approved by the publishing company. Only then is it published. Then you have kindle and that opens another can of worms.

The fallowing novels are unpublished as I write this but will be published soon. Keep checking Amazom.com for any new novels that I have published. Everything that I publish is also on Kindle.

1. "The Mountain Ghost."
   The Legend of Russell Blake.
   After the Chinese and North Koreans attack the southern United States two young brothers, Brandon and Russell Blake go after the invading enemy. After Brandon is killed Russell smears a white past allover his exposed skin and earns the name Mountain Ghost.

2. The Mountain Ghost."
   Making of a Legend
   The Mountain Ghost continues to fight the Chinese and North Koreans soldiers that have invaded

the entire southern half of the United States.

3. "The Mountain Ghost."
The Ghost Soldiers.
After the death of Russell Black his son, Russ, continues as to bring death and destruction to the enemy as the new Mountain Ghost.

4. "The Mountain Ghost."
The Ghost Warriors.
After Russ and June have twin girls they grow up and move back south to fight the Chinese and North Koreans as the Ghost Twins. Before long they grow in numbers and call themselves the Ghost Warriors.

5. "The Glassy War."
Three thousand years in the future and three galaxies away the

United Planet Counsel fight and enemy that is trying to control every galaxy they come to. After both starships crash into the planet the survivors continue to fight.

6. "The Fire Dancers."

I stopped writing this novel to start writing the Mountain Ghost series but I will be getting back to it.

I hope that you have enjoyed this novel. Please help me by sending your comments on what you thought about this novel or book by e-mailing me at bubbasbooks@msn.com . By doing this you will help me to be a better writer. You will also let me know what you, the public, is looking for in these types of novels and books. I have a very creative mind, a bit warped some say but, still creative but, I still need to know what you are looking for. I thank you for your assistance in this.

Vernon Gillen